HOW TO BECOME A PROCESS SERVER

PROCESS SERVER 101

HOW TO BECOME A PROCESS SERVER

BY RICHARD YOUNG

ISBN: 978-1-79-876976-8

This book wouldn't be possible without the many process servers over the years who've shared their successes and challenges. Thank you.

Table of Contents

The $1,000 a Day Process Server

Since 2012, I've run a popular blog for process servers based on my own experience starting a process server business from my home office in Colorado.

In that time, I've received thousands of emails and comments from people who want to become a self-employed process server.

Unfortunately, there's a lot of bad information on the Internet, some even meant to discourage people from getting started in the industry.

I've created this concise little book to set the record straight, and to assure you there's never been a better time to become a process server and start your own business.

With the advantages of modern technology it's easier than ever, and you won't need much more than your smartphone and a stack of business cards to get started.

In fact, I specifically recommend against investing much money into your business until you're already making a profit.

Let's take a look at what you'll learn:

1) We'll start with the very basics, covering key concepts such as licensing and legal requirements, personal and substituted service, and court filing.

2) Once you've mastered the basics, we'll take a look at setting up a professional business that inspires confidence in your clients.

3) From there we'll cover marketing and promotion, including the simplest way to find your first client and how to promote your business without selling or cold-calling (because everyone hates cold-calling).

But first, I'd like to share the story of the $1,000 a day process server:

Steve wanted to become a process server so he didn't have to sell the best years of his life to a blood-sucking corporation.

He ordered a stack of shiny business cards and all the latest gadgets, and spent hours researching civil process and case law.

But the clients only trickled in.

Steve never built the business he wanted, and I imagine he's now working a regular job somewhere (not everyone is cut out for self-employment).

What went wrong?

Steve pursued his dream and put a lot of effort into making it successful.

But his problem wasn't working hard; his problem was working hard in all the wrong places.

And as the business failed, Steve became desperate.

The few clients he'd managed to attract began to sense his desperation and jumped ship (there's a reason they call lawyers sharks—they can sense desperation better than a 14-foot great white).

When I tried to help guide him in the right direction, Steve got defensive and wrote me a long email about how the whole industry must be a scam.

And I never heard from him again.

Now let's talk about Carlos:

Like Steve, Carlos wanted to become a process server and work for himself.

He jumped right in, pursuing clients from day one, and went after them with a ferociousness I've rarely seen.

And was Carlos desperate?

Did he lowball his rates and kill his business?

Just the opposite: Carlos set his fees above-market and when things got too busy he raised them even higher.

Was he worried about losing clients?

Of course not.

New referrals were lining up and the clients happy to pay his rates were usually easier to work with (more on that later).

The last time I heard from Carlos he told me he was making $1,000 or more on a busy day.

And he hasn't emailed since.

I figured he's too busy making money.

What did Carlos do that's so different from Steve?

And how can you apply his success to your new process server business?

Carlos focused his energy in the right places.

He wasn't worried about knowing every obscure piece of case law.

And he didn't let his doubts and insecurities get the best of him.

Instead, he focused on finding and attracting clients (because without clients you're not in business).

He built a website (it's easy and I'll walk you through it step-by-step).

He passed out business cards and marketing letters.

And with plenty of clients and money coming in, the rest fell into place.

Here's the real secret:

You don't need any experience, a fancy degree, or a lot of money to become a process server (you can even start part-time while you keep your day job).

Instead, you're going to figure things out as you go, without knowing every little detail or fact about the industry.

Without knowing every law and statute in the books.

Without a masterclass in civil procedure.

And without fancy and expensive equipment.

Yes, it's scary.

But it's the only way.

I promise.

Time and time again I've watched new process servers struggle and fail before they even get past the first step.

They send me long emails with every obscure question and legal issue they can conjure up.

And they waste their own time thinking they need to be a legal expert to become a process server.

It's simple:

1) Client gives you the papers.

2) Serve them according to the rules of civil procedure in your state (it's not complicated, and I'll show you where to find all of the information you need).

3) Sign and file the return of service or deliver it to the client (again, it's very simple, and if you get stuck the folks at the courthouse are a helpful resource).

4) Get paid.

That's all there is to it!

Of course, there are some important details along the way.

Have confidence you can figure them out as you go, and don't be like the newbies who get bogged down in endless research before they even get started (I sometimes think these people don't actually want to become process servers —they're more in love with the idea of self-employment and are happy to whittle their life away on Google and useless message boards).

Now it's time to let you in on one of my own secrets:

I got started the same way, almost by accident.

A co-worker needed some divorce papers served on his soon-to-be ex-wife and I agreed to help him out.

I had no idea what I was doing.

But I was determined to figure things out along the way.

I'll never forget that feeling of serving my first papers.

In fact, my hands were shaking so badly, I'm pretty sure I was more nervous than the defendant.

But the whole thing was over in less than five minutes.

Was it scary?

I'd be lying if I said it wasn't.

But I learned more about process serving in my very first case than most newbies who never make it past the "research" phase.

And a week later I got another call from my co-worker.

Turns out a friend of his also needed a good process server, and he knew just the right person for the job.

A business was born.

And the rest is history.

In business, as in life, there are dreamers and there are "doers."

And the doers are the ones making progress, learning from their mistakes, and getting things done.

But now, something I've been dying to clear up:

There's a nasty myth floating around the process server community that you have to be an "insider" to be successful.

Fathers teach the business to their sons.

Families work together to protect their closely guarded secrets, and no outsider has a shot in hell at getting their foot in the door.

This is bullshit.

Clients don't care who your daddy is.

All they care about is getting their papers served in a timely manner by someone trustworthy and reliable.

Be that person and you'll have all the business you can handle.

There are no secret circles, no illuminati of process servers.

The field is open to all who wish to play.

Job vs. Self-Employment

Before we can cover the basics of service of process, it's important to decide which kind of process server you would like to become.

There are two main categories of process servers:

Those who work for someone else, either as a regular employee or independent contractor, and those who own their own business.

Most process servers work as independent contractors for existing process server agencies.

You'll see these positions advertised on job boards, Craigslist, or in the local newspaper.

The requirements are often low, and it's fairly easy to get started.

The biggest advantage is that the agency supplies the work. You won't need to worry about running a business or finding clients, and it can be a good way to get some experience before pursuing self-employment.

However, the pay is often quite low, usually about $12-$15 per serve, which means you'll need to serve a lot of papers every day in order to make a living.

As with any job, the lion's share of the revenue is kept by the owner, while they pay you only a small fraction of the revenue.

And there are some additional drawbacks:

1) For tax purposes you'll be classified as an independent contractor and will have to withhold and file your own taxes. Essentially, you're in business for yourself and a small mistake could mean owing Uncle Sam a lot of money at the end of the year.

2) You lack the security of a traditional job. If the agency you work for loses clients and there's no work, your income will take a hit.

3) Benefits are usually not provided, which means you'll need to buy your own health insurance (and you can forget about paid vacations or sick days).

4) In most cases, you'll need to provide your own smartphone and transportation (including the cost of fuel and repairs).

The alternative to working for someone else is self-employment, and it's easier than you might think to start your own process server business.

While you're still responsible for covering your expenses and withholding your own taxes, you get to keep 100% of the fees you charge, so you have the potential to make a lot more money with less work.

Here's a quick example:

Let's suppose you work for a process server agency who pays you $15 per serve.

In order to make $200 per day you would need to serve at least 13 papers.

That's a lot of fuel and time spent driving all over town (and remember that it often takes more than one attempt to complete a serve).

Now imagine you work for yourself and bill your clients just $50 per serve.

You would only need to serve 4 papers a day to make the same amount of money.

In fact, you could work part-time while keeping your day job (at least in the beginning) and still make more than most people do in a day.

The choice is obvious to me.

But as the saying goes, with great power comes great responsibility.

And self-employment just isn't for everyone.

If you're overwhelmed by the prospect of promoting your business and finding clients, then perhaps working for someone is a good way to test the waters.

But if you're like me, and you crave the freedom that comes from working for yourself, then it's worth the effort.

This book is for you.

Service of Process

We live in a great country.

We have a system of laws that ensures everyone's rights are upheld, and the process server is part of that system.

There's a nasty stereotype that persists about people hiding from process servers.

Imagine some poor soul huddled in their bedroom closet while the process server pounds on their front door—or the process server showing up in disguise at the most inopportune moment, delivering the bad news with gusto and flair upon our unsuspecting victim.

This is bogus.

You see, one important principle in our system of laws is that the defendant in any legal action has a right to be notified of the charges against them.

And it's the process server who guarantees that right.

While we work for and are paid by the plaintiff in the case, it's the defendant's rights we are working to protect.

And that's why it's vitally important we're impartial third parties, with no interests in the case, and why we must always conduct ourselves with integrity.

So while there's a popular misconception that we're the bad guys, we're actually working on the side of justice.

Without process servers, the whole system falls apart.

What Process Servers Do

While there's certainly a mystery that surrounds process servers and the work we do, most of the time it's pretty simple.

A client gives us a call when they have papers to be served, and we either pick the papers up or receive them by fax, email, or some other electronic means.

The defendant's name (the person we are going to serve), and in most cases their last known address, will be listed.

It's our job to find that person and serve them the papers.

This is done according to the rules of civil procedure in each state or U.S. territory (plus the District of Columbia).

Once the papers are served, the process server completes a "return or service," also called a proof of service or affidavit of service, which affirms that the papers were served to the defendant by the process server.

We then deliver the return of service to the client or file it with the court of jurisdiction (the court where the case was originally filed) on their behalf.

Last, but certainly not least, the client pays us for our work.

Sounds simple, right?

That's because it is, and you as the process server have a tremendous amount of flexibility with how you run your business and make your serves—so long as you're following the rules of civil procedure in your state.

Of course, it's never quite as simple as it seems.

Sometimes the defendant isn't home, no longer lives at the same address, or they deliberately avoid being served.

We spend an awful lot of time driving or waiting around, and sometimes resort to some pretty creative measures to make a serve (more on that later).

But first, let's take a look at the requirements to work as a process server.

Legal Requirements

The majority of U.S. states and territories don't license process servers.

Anyone over the age of 18 (in a few cases 21) and who is not a party to the case may serve legal process.

If you happen to live in one of these states, you can get started as a process server without jumping through hoops, and can move right on to promoting your business and finding clients (I'll give you plenty of ideas for promoting your business later in the book).

If you do live in a state that licenses or otherwise regulates process servers, don't despair.

The requirements are often simple and if you take them one at a time you'll be serving papers before you know it.

For example, California requires process servers who complete more than 10 serves a year to register, and in order to register you'll need to pass a background check (no felony convictions) and post a $2,000 bond.

While $2,000 might sound like a lot of money, a California process server bond can be purchased online for $50-$100.

If you're not sure of the requirements in your state, I've posted a list of the requirements on my website:

https://www.processserver101.com

However, laws and legal requirements are subject to change and I always recommend checking with your state or local jurisdiction for the latest requirements.

And while you're at it, go ahead and Google your state's rules of civil procedure.

Yes, they're long (sometimes even hundreds or thousands of pages), but the only part we're focused on is service of process.

These are the basic guidelines that every process server in your state must follow; who can serve papers, how they should be served, and how proof of service should be filed with the court.

I recommend printing the section on service of process because you're going to refer to it a lot in your career, particularly while you're new and learning the ropes.

At the very least you should familiarize yourself with the basics.

As we move forward and talk about the different types of service, I'll remind you to refer back to your state's rules.

Personal Service

Personal service is the most common method used by process servers.

In short, personal service is when we physically hand the papers to the defendant, and it's what most people imagine when they think of a process server.

But we're not always serving an individual.

Sometimes we're serving a business, a government agency, or even your state's attorney general, and this still falls under the category of personal service.

In the case of a business, you'll either serve a manager, corporate officer, or some other responsible party.

Some states will even permit you to serve a security officer or the receptionist in the lobby if you can be reasonably sure that person will pass along the papers to a responsible party.

But what if a business doesn't maintain a regular office?

In that case, you're going to serve their registered agent.

A registered agent is a party who agrees to receive service of process on behalf of a company, and they must maintain a physical address where service can be made.

You can find a business's registered agent by checking with your secretary of state's office (or whichever government agency registers businesses in your state).

The information is public record and is usually searchable online.

Serving a government agency is even easier, because they maintain regular office hours and usually have an employee on site who's responsible for receiving service of process.

Three things to keep in mind when making personal service:

1) It's important to identify your subject. Usually I do this simply by stating their name and waiting for them to respond. Alternatively, you could look them up on Google or social media and find a clear picture before you attempt service.

2) Contrary to what the movies portray, we don't actually say, "You've been served!" It's unnecessary and in some cases will only agitate your subject, potentially resulting in a confrontation. It's enough to simply inform them that you have some important legal documents to give them.

3) In the event they refuse to accept the papers, this is what we call a refusal of service. As long as you've properly identified the subject it's okay to leave the papers at their feet or on the doorstep. Their refusal

to physically take the document does not mean it's not a valid serve. For more clarity on refusal of service, be sure to check your state's rules of civil procedure.

Substituted Service

Substituted service is a tricky area, and you will need to confirm your state's individual rules on what qualifies as a valid serve.

Generally speaking, substituted service occurs when we do not serve the party named as the defendant, but instead serve someone on their behalf.

This could be another adult residing at the same address, such as a spouse, roommate, or in some states, even a child as young as thirteen.

Substituted service may also occur when we serve process by some other means, such as certified mail, newspaper publication, email, or even service by social media.

Your state may have specific guidelines for substituted service, but in the case of a defendant who is repeatedly avoiding service or simply cannot be located, the individual judge in the case may decide which form of substituted service they're willing to accept.

In these difficult cases, it's important to consult with your client regarding the steps you've taken to complete service and the additional options that might be available.

Return of Service

A return of service, sometimes called a proof of service or affidavit of service, is the document the process server returns to the client certifying that service of process has been made.

It's a simple form, with the case number and court of jurisdiction, the defendant's name and address, and a section for the process server to sign and complete.

It's extremely important to complete an accurate return of service because this document is filed with the court and becomes a permanent part of the case record.

Falsifying a return of service is unethical, damages the reputation of our profession, and could result in severe civil or even criminal charges being filed against you.

Keep in mind that in most jurisdictions (such as my home state of Colorado), all return of service forms in civil cases are notarized, making them legal affidavits. Knowingly falsifying an affidavit is considered perjury and will be treated as such by the courts.

Consider establishing a good relationship with a notary, because you'll be using their services a lot. Some process servers charge the client an extra fee for notarization, but I build the expense into my standard fee to keep things as simple as possible for the client.

Usually, the return of service form is supplied by the client. In the case of law firms, they'll almost always provide this form to the process server—with the case number and relevant information already filled in.

Legal document preparation services and self-help kits (such as those used in divorce cases by people who cannot afford an attorney), typically also provide a return of service form.

If you're working with a client who does not provide a return a service form, you can use a generic form and add the important details.

For a list of generic process server forms, visit my website and click on each state:

https://www.processserver101.com/process-server-laws

Another option is to use the free affidavit of service generator from RocketLawyer.

Simply fill in the case details and the generator will create a ready-to-print form you can sign and return to the client.

Here's the link:

https://www.rocketlawyer.com/document/affidavit-of-service.rl#/

If you decide to create a free account, take good care to protect your password.

While the return of service ultimately becomes a part of the public court record, we have a duty as process servers to respect and protect the confidentiality of our clients.

Court Filing

Depending on the needs of your client, you'll either return your completed proof of service to them or file it on their behalf.

Many law firms choose to do their own filings, as do most private individuals who hire a process server, but some will elect to have you file the return of service for them.

This is an extra service and you should bill an additional fee for court filing.

While it might sound complicated, court filing is actually quite simple.

The old school method is to visit the clerk's office at the courthouse where the case is filed. Just let them know you have a return or affidavit of service to file and they'll know exactly what to do.

Make sure you get a receipt for your client's records.

It's worth noting that the clerks at the courthouse, while often overworked, are usually quite friendly and you'll want to build a good relationship with them. They know a lot about procedure and if you ever get stuck wondering how to complete a return of service or where to file, they're great at pointing you in the right direction.

Like everything these days, most courts have also adopted electronic filing. This means that with a cheap portable scanner you can file an electronic copy of the return of service, and send a copy to your client along with the filing receipt. There's no need to drive to your client's office or the courthouse, saving you a lot of gas and time.

Unfortunately, there's no universal system for electronic filing, and each court system maintains their own requirements and procedures.

It's worth checking with the courts in your area to familiarize yourself with their filing requirements, and you can usually find the information you need on their websites.

Skip Tracing

Okay, let's take a break from the boring legal stuff and talk about something that always gets process servers excited.

Skip tracing.

I'm sure you're familiar with the term, but in case you're not, let's break it down:

People move.

They disappear.

And sometimes they go to great lengths to avoid being found by process servers, bill collectors, law enforcement, or anyone looking to find them.

The art and science of tracking these people down is called skip tracing.

Learn the essentials, and it's an additional service you to offer your clients for those tough-to-serve cases.

In fact, process servers who do skip tracing can bill extra for it, sometimes $30-$50 per hour or more.

So it's worth adding some good skip tracing techniques to your bag of tricks.

In the 21st century, social media had become the process server or private investigator's go-to source for locating people.

It's astonishing what people will put on the Internet.

I remember one case where the defendant no longer lived at their last known address, and nobody, from the neighbors to the landlord, had any good information about where he might have moved.

But I watched his social media profiles, and it didn't take long to figure out he was going to the same gym almost daily.

So I posted up in the parking lot with his photo still fresh in my mind, settled in with a coffee and a bagel, and waited.

Not more than two hours later I spotted him leaving a black Jeep, strolling towards the entrance of the gym without a care in the world.

And just like that I completed my serve.

The client, who had hired two previous process servers with no luck, was so happy they gave me all of their business from that point forward.

It was so easy I almost felt guilty (okay, I said almost).

In addition to social media, we've got other digital resources to rely upon in our search for the elusive defendant.

But my favorite, and the one I use now almost exclusively, is Pipl:

https://pipl.com

Pipl is a deep-web search engine that combines public records with social networks, professional sites, lifestyle sites, phone directories, and marketing lists to return a complete profile on an individual.

All you need is one data point, like a name or email address, and it's amazing what Pipl will find.

You'll get a complete list of social media profiles, previous addresses, business contacts, work history, and even known relatives.

And while it's not always going to help you immediately locate your subject, having a list of where they've lived before, in addition to known relatives, gives you a head-start for some good old fashioned, boots on the ground skip tracing.

In fact, one my favorite places to turn is the defendant's mother, because when people are in trouble and at their most desperate, they always run home to mom.

In more than one case I've been able to locate the defendant at the mother's address.

And if they're not there, mom often knows where they're staying.

Usually I explain to the mother that I'm a process server, not a police officer, and that I'm not looking to arrest their child.

If the mom is sensible, she's going to help you out, because most people understand that legal problems won't simply go away by avoiding the process server.

But my favorite technique, by and large, is to find out where the defendant is working.

This is one of the reasons I love working divorce cases. Usually the spouse knows exactly where the other works, and can even provide their work schedule.

Serving people at work has distinct advantages.

Unlike a residence, where the defendant may very well have access to some kind of firearm or weapon, people most likely don't take a gun with them to work.

And the social pressure and desire to maintain a positive relationship with their employer helps to keep a person's attitude and anger in check.

Don't make a scene, be discreet and respectful, and they'll usually accept the papers with a silent nod.

Personal Safety

In a general sense, process serving is a relatively safe profession.

In fact, it doesn't even crack the top ten list of most dangerous occupations.

You're at higher risk for assault and personal injury as a nurse, firefighter, or convenience store clerk.

By far the biggest risk to process servers is simply the amount of time we spend in a vehicle. Making sure your transportation is safe, with good brakes, air in the tires, and working seat belts goes a long way.

But we can and do come into contact with agitated or distressed individuals, and it's worth taking a few precautions to increase your personal safety.

If you have any hesitations about the history of the individual you're serving, you can always run a simple background check.

Most court records and arrest histories will come up with a quick Google search, or you can check your state's court or correctional websites.

There have been times when I'm aware of a person's violent past, and I've brought along a friend or two for extra support. They wait in the car, observe what happens, and can call for help quickly if there's a problem.

You can even request a "civil standby" from local law enforcement if your subject has a particularly disturbing history of violence.

Fortunately, I've never had a serve escalate into a physical confrontation, but I'm still not above asking for help when I need it.

As a hard rule, you should never engage in a shouting match or argue with an aggressive person.

We're here to do a job and get paid, not to prove how tough we are.

I'd be lying if I said I didn't sometimes want to respond to the occasional curse or verbal threat hurled my way by an upset defendant, but I always manage to stay professional, complete my serve, and leave quickly.

Which brings me to another point:

It's often advantageous not to look or act like a law enforcement officer.

This always comes up with the subject of process server badges.

As long as you're not impersonating a law enforcement officer, and there's no local law restricting the use of badges, process servers can and often do wear badges.

In fact, I have a personalized badge that I've worn while making serves.

But it's important to consider the context.

Think about it like this:

Imagine you're a defendant trying to avoid service.

If you see someone wearing a badge walking up to the front door, would you answer it?

Of course not.

In the wrong neighborhood, a process server wearing a badge can bring a lot of unwanted and negative attention, or the neighbors could even alert the defendant of your approach.

And sometimes process servers who insist on wearing a badge make things a lot harder for themselves.

It's much easier to approach the defendant without a badge, authority demeanor, or any of the usual telltale signs of law enforcement.

That's why I'm most successful making serves in jeans and a t-shirt; sometimes I even wear shorts.

But I always avoid setting off those red flags.

With that said, there are certainly times when wearing a badge can make things easier, like when serving process in a corporate or government office building.

And in the rare event that a situation escalates and law enforcement responds to the scene, a badge can help identify your position.

I like to wear mine under my shirt on a chain with a leather badge holder.

It's ready when I need it, hidden when I don't.

In the past, I've been asked by new process servers if they should carry any personal protection devices or a firearm when making serves.

My answer is that I'm generally opposed to it, but it's a personal choice each process server must make for themselves.

I've always found my best defense was simply to walk away and avoid problems before they escalate.

Whatever decision you make, it goes without saying that you should do your research and always comply with local laws.

For more information about process server assault and safety, I recommend visiting the website of the PAAPRS Safety Campaign.

They're working to document and reduce the number of assaults on process servers, and are actively campaigning to make assaulting a process server a felony in all fifty states (you can even add your name to the petition).

Here's the link:

https://www.serve-now.com/resources/paaprs

Difficult Serves

From time to time you'll have a defendant who does everything in their power to avoid service.

Perhaps you've located their residence, but they simply refuse to come to the door and keep the blinds drawn tightly shut at all hours of the day.

As a process server, you're going to encounter these situations, and you'll need to flex some creative muscle in order to overcome the challenges and complete those difficult serves.

I'm reminded of a case I once worked.

It started out simple enough.

I'd done some work for the client before and they always did their homework, so I knew the defendant's address was good.

And through some simple snooping, I found out he owned a small business registered to the same address. His work truck was parked outside the residence.

But no matter how many times I rang the bell he wouldn't answer the door.

I tried at all hours of the day with no luck.

I even waited down the street for several hours one morning, in the hopes of catching him as he left for work.

But I just couldn't make the serve.

The place was sealed up tighter than Fort Knox.

So I turned to one of my favorite tricks, and mailed him a small package full of gummy worms with signature confirmation from the post office.

Why gummy worms?

I don't know, maybe I thought it was funny.

From my snooping and surveillance I knew what time the mail was delivered each day, so once again I waited down the street.

When the letter carrier approached the front door I followed shortly behind him—just off to one side to avoid being seen.

The defendant opened the door wide, confirmed his identity, and signed for the package.

At just the right moment I swooped in to drop the papers at his feet.

I'll never forget the look of surprise on the guy's face.

Long story short, my client was thrilled with the results and gave me a lot more work down the line.

And mailing gummy worms became something of a tradition for me.

But hey, it works.

Never forget that this is your business, and you have a lot of flexibility to make your serves however you like, just as long as you stick to the rules of civil procedure and don't break any laws.

While I don't personally prefer to use disguises, I'm not above throwing on a brown polo shirt to look like a delivery driver, or catching someone on their way to buy groceries.

One time, I even found out where the defendant liked to drink on the weekends and served them at their neighborhood bar (they'd posted regular photos on social media).

But remember, when a serve gets difficult, and you're going to resort to creative and time-consuming measures, you should always check with your client for approval before billing them for surveillance and stakeouts.

Most are happy to pay, particularly if they've run out of luck with other process servers, but some would rather go back to the judge and pursue alternative options such as service by mail or publication.

Ethics for Process Servers

I won't bore you with a long lecture about ethics, but it's critical to our industry—and especially to the clients you'll be working with—that you always conduct yourself at the highest levels of professionalism.

There's a dirty little problem in our business called sewer service.

Just in case you haven't heard the term before, it's when a process server says they've served papers when in fact they actually haven't, in order to get paid for work they didn't do.

It usually goes something like this:

A process server working as an independent contractor for a large agency figures out quickly that they're not going to make much money getting paid $15 per serve.

So instead of doing things properly, they slide papers under doors or leave them on front porches without confirming the defendant still lives at the address.

They sign the proof of service, return everything to their boss, and go home thinking about how clever they are.

But eventually, one or two of those defendants end up contesting the service in court and the case is thrown out or delayed.

And pretty soon the clever process server is getting served themselves, because they've cost their clients a lot of time and money.

They could even end up with criminal charges filed against them, because falsifying an affidavit of service is perjury and is subject to criminal penalties.

While the majority of process servers are honest and hardworking people, a story like this crops up from time to time and it damages the reputation of our industry (all you have to do is Google "process server sewer service" and you'll find dozens of high profile news stories).

Remember, when you sign your name to a proof of service you are certifying to the court that service was made in accordance with the law, and your signature ultimately becomes a part of the permanent case record.

While it may seem easy to cut corners, it's simply not worth the loss of your business, a civil suit, or criminal charges.

But what if you're not sure about a serve?

Maybe you saw the defendant through a window and slid the papers under the door after they refused your repeated attempts, or you can't be certain the roommate you served will actually pass along the papers.

What then?

As process servers we must rely on the legal principle of "reasonable standards."

It's the same legal principle applied to a diverse range of cases, from justified self-defense to medical malpractice.

In other words, would a reasonable person in the same situation believe the papers were served properly?

Could you explain, in a way any reasonable person would understand, why you considered your serve to be valid?

If so, you can sign your name to the proof of service and file it with the court.

If not, you need to reconsider your options for effecting a proper serve.

While I certainly hope you're never called to defend yourself before a judge or court, it's certainly a possibility.

That's why it's so important to conduct yourself with professional integrity.

It's worth the peace of mind to do things the right way and never take shortcuts with your livelihood.

Setting Up Your Business

Process serving is a cheap business to get into.

Dirt cheap.

All you really need is a stack of business cards, a cell phone, and reliable transportation (I would also recommend you build a website—more on that later).

In fact, my third (and biggest) client came from a ten cent business card passed along by the co-worker who hired me to serve his wife (now ex-wife).

That cheap little business card landed me a steady stream of work and earned its weight in gold many time over.

But like the newbies who lose themselves in endless legal research, there are those who think they must acquire every gadget and gizmo under the sun before they can start their business.

Before they know it, they've spent their entire startup budget and they still don't have a single client.

I get it.

Gadgets are cool, but there's plenty of time for that.

For now, it's enough to focus on the basic essentials you need to get your business off the ground.

Legal Structure

Of course, doing business means you'll need some sort of legal structure.

In addition to complying with the law, a proper legal structure allows you to open a business bank account and accept payments in your business's name.

Most independent process servers operate as a sole proprietorship or limited liability company (LLC).

Here's the difference:

1) A sole proprietorship means that you will conduct business under a separate trade name (such as *Your Process Server Business*), but ultimately you as the owner are responsible for all financial obligations, including whatever debts your business might take on. That means if you default on the debt later, your creditors can come after not only the business but also your personal accounts. However, the tiny overhead and startup expenses mean most process servers don't accrue debt to start their business, and the low fees and simple requirements for a sole proprietorship make it an attractive option (last time I checked a sole proprietorship in my home state could be filed with a simple online form, and costs just $20 for the first year and $5 a year thereafter).

2) Limited liability companies are the next step above a sole proprietorship, and can help to limit your personal liability in the event the business takes on debt. Like a sole proprietorship, LLC's can often be filed online, though they may have additional annual reporting and filing requirements. You may also choose to be taxed as an individual, reporting your profits and expenses on your personal tax return, or the LLC may elect to be taxed as a corporation.

To find more specific information, I recommend visiting your state's website and reading more about the registration and filing requirements for small businesses.

Another great source of information is the Small Business Administration:

https://www.sba.gov

Local Business Requirements

It's also worth taking a look at the local business licensing requirements in your state or town.

In most cases, you won't need a local business license if you're conducting business from your home, though some municipalities do require even home-based businesses to register.

Your city or county should have the current requirements posted on their website.

A Free, Professional Phone Number

One of the things I love most about the process server business is that the overhead is so minimal.

You don't need a fancy office, receptionist, retail space, or the expensive equipment that can bury most small businesses before they even get started.

In fact, you can pretty much run this business from your smartphone.

However, I do recommend setting up a professional office number for your business that forwards calls to your personal phone.

That way, if you decide you switch numbers or want to share the call load with your partner, you'll have a dedicated number to give your clients.

And instead of listing your personal number on your business cards or website you can list your business number to maintain a degree of privacy.

Fortunately, you can get a dedicated number for free from Google Voice.

When you want to take a day off, you can even tell Google Voice to take a voicemail and email or text you a transcript of the message.

Here's the link:

https://voice.google.com

Sending & Receiving Faxes

Fax machines are dead.

At least I thought they were dead.

For some reason, lawyers still love them, and occasionally you'll get an old-school type who wants to fax you paperwork.

If you can't delicately convince them to send you an email attachment, you can send or receive a limited amount of faxes from your desktop or mobile device using FaxBurner's free service.

The downside is that you won't have a permanent fax number, so if you need to send faxes regularly you'll have to upgrade to the premium subscription.

Still, at $9.97 a month it's a lot cheaper than a clunky fax machine and dedicated phone line.

Take a look:

https://www.faxburner.com

Custom Email Address

I strongly recommend you create a custom email address for your business.

Which looks more professional?

yourcompany@gmail.com

Or…

yourname@yourcompany.com

Having a custom email address adds a professional touch and has become essential for any small business owner.

In order to get a custom email address, you'll first need a domain name for your business (for example: www.yourbusiness.com).

If you don't already have one, I recommend you purchase a domain name when you setup your website, so that's it pre-configured and ready to use.

Of course, you could pay Google or some other premium service $5-$10 a month for a custom email address, but you can easily add one when build your website the way I recommend in the next chapter.

Promoting Your Business

You're not really a process server until you serve your first papers.

And you can't serve your first papers without a client.

If you spend too much time on the details and not enough time finding clients, your business will go nowhere.

So who hires process servers?

Basically, our clients fall into one of two categories:

1) Private individuals who need a process server for one case. These are often divorce or small claims cases, and the client is working with a self-help document preparation center or a no-frills attorney. When it's time for their papers to be served, they look for a process server. I'm happy to serve these clients, but they rarely result in repeat business.

2) Attorneys, landlords, and corporations who regularly file legal actions such as lawsuits or evictions. This is the bread and butter of our business, because if you can form a relationship with these clients they'll generate a lot of repeat work.

While I do recommend leaving some of your business cards with the local self-help document preparation centers (so they can pass them along to their clients who need a process server), the second category is where you should be focusing your marketing efforts.

It's the full-service divorce attorneys, real estate attorneys, landlords, and collection agencies that will generate the most work.

What Clients Really Want

I'm going to let you in on another secret:

Unfortunately, there are a lot of really bad process servers out there.

At best, they fail to follow up and bounce from client to client.

At worst, they act like tough guys and get a kick out of banging on people's doors.

You know the type.

They've got all the latest tactical gear and read Soldier of Fortune magazine.

Let me tell you, attorneys hate these types.

They're a liability.

And there's nothing attorneys hate more than liability.

Imagine for a moment you're a lawyer:

You've spent weeks, maybe even months, preparing a big case and now you've got to hand the paperwork over to a process server.

Everything rests on this person's ability to do the job.

Do you want a tough guy, or do you want someone reliable, smart, who can be counted on to serve your case with ethics and integrity?

Of course, the choice is obvious.

Fortunately for us, these bad or just plain incompetent process servers create an opportunity, because if you inspire confidence in your clients and act with intelligence they'll choose you every time.

But don't get me wrong, not all process servers are incompetent.

In fact, it's quite the opposite.

Our industry is filled with diligent, honest, hard-working people who give it their best every day.

So how do you compete in such a market?

The single most effective way to differentiate yourself from the competition is to be expensive.

Resist the urge new process servers have to set their rates too low.

In most cases, law firms don't even pay for the process server.

They pass the expense along to the client and may even charge more than what the process server bills, making a profit from the difference.

Attorneys don't care what you charge per serve.

What they care about is getting their case served in a reliable, timely manner by a professional.

When you set your prices too low, it looks needy and amateurish.

It's a red flag.

Believe me, attorneys can spot needy people.

Above-average rates project confidence and a full schedule.

You'll also attract better clients who appreciate your time and personal attention.

But it goes beyond the client:

To make $200 a day at $35 a serve, you would have to make six serves per day.

At $70 per serve you only have to make three good serves to break $200.

That's half the drive-time, half the gas money, and half the effort to make the same amount of money.

So even if you charge more and serve less papers you can still come out on top.

Know Your Competition

Here's something you can do in the next thirty minutes:

Head over to Google and search for process servers in your town.

Spend half an hour exploring what other process servers in your area are doing with their businesses.

Have fun. Who doesn't love a little harmless snooping?

You'll likely find a range of businesses from high-volume firms with multiple employees (or contractors) to single-person operations being run from a home office.

Here are some things to note:

1) The types of service each company offers.

2) Whether or not they post their rates online—if so, what are they?

3) Features of each website that you find appealing—which ones improve the company's image and which make it worse?

4) How are the process servers building trust? Is it effective? If not, what makes them seem untrustworthy?

5) Do they include a phone number or a contact form?

6) Are they using client references and testimonials? Do they have any photos? Do they hurt or help their image?

7) And anything else you find noteworthy or compelling.

The goal is to understand your playing field. That way, you can stand out from what others are doing and develop your own position in the market.

One example of this is what Apple did with the iPod.

Before the iPod we all carried those big floppy CD cases (I remember bragging to friends about having 240 CD's in my car).

And before that we had tapes and records.

I'm not saying there weren't other .mp3 players when Apple released the iPod. There were. But most of them were unreliable and cheaply made. And the software needed to "sync up" was usually pretty spotty.

Apple saw a hole and filled it.

They made it easy for the average, non-technical person to download an album and have it playing from their iPod in minutes.

And people loved it.

Although the marketplace has shifted and Apple has many emerging competitors, their position as the innovator behind the iPod contributes to their brand today.

Even the massive success of the iPhone can be traced to the now-humble iPod. It set the tone for things to come.

The process server market in your area is no different.

It has gaping holes just waiting to be filled. As you survey your competitors, consider how you might fill one of those gaps.

Take ten minutes and brainstorm a short list of the unique strengths and advantages you can bring to your business.

Also, consider how those strengths can benefit your clients.

Do you have a background in customer service? Then offer the best service in town.

Are you experienced in a similar field? Maybe you're a veteran or retired police officer?

Or perhaps your strength and tenacity come from being a single mom.

It's going to be different for everyone.

You've just got to be creative and dig a little.

Crafting Your Unique Selling Proposition

Suppose you're at home watching the boob tube and enjoying your favorite take-out.

Crunch!

Suddenly, you bite something hard. Really hard. Pain sets in...then more pain.

First it's just your tooth, but within moments it's spread through your jaw.

Your eyes are watering.

Your head is pounding.

It's awful.

Who do you want to call?

The cosmetic dentist who promises "a million-dollar smile" in his ads?

Or how about "the friendliest dentist in town?"

They're not terrible choices.

Both might be able to help you (good luck getting the cosmetic dentist on the phone after five o'clock).

But imagine you spot the following ad:

Severe tooth pain? I can help.
Emergency and after-hours dentistry.
Call Dr. John Cavitt: 303-555-0168

How does that strike you in the moment?

If it were me, Dr. Cavitt is who I would call because his unique selling proposition (help with severe tooth pain) appeals to my urgent need at that exact moment.

So what is a unique selling proposition?

Think of it as what you're known for.

It tells a potential client what you're all about and what you're going to do for them.

Think back to the example of the dentists.

They've all been to dental school.

But each one presents their business in a unique way to feature their strengths and attracts the clients who are looking for what they offer.

Simple, right?

Take the list of strengths you brainstormed earlier and use them to craft a unique selling proposition of your own.

It's a common mistake to think including your personal touch makes something unprofessional.

In fact, the exact opposite is usually true.

Giving the clients a real person to connect with goes a long way towards building trust and it's central to creating a business you'll love as much as your clients do.

I once met two process servers in Denver who were both veterans, so they worked that into their USP. They feature their military service prominently and target attorneys who've also served. It's unique, it's who they are, and it builds trust.

One of my favorite stories is the San Francisco process server who pedaled from law firm to law firm on his bike billing himself as "San Francisco's Greenest Process Server."

In San Francisco (known for progressive politics), he appealed to a whole bunch of "do-good" attorneys and did quite well. Not only did he meet their primary need (reliably serving papers) but he did so in a way that was memorable and appealing to his clients.

Success comes from satisfying your client's needs in a way that no other process server can.

Scratch that itch and you'll have clients coming back for years to come.

Marketing Letters

One question I've heard over and over is, "What's the best way to get my first client?"

The fastest, cheapest, and most direct way to get your first client is to introduce yourself directly to law firms in your area.

Law firms are the bread and butter of our business. A small firm might only need you here and there, but a large firm could produce dozens of papers to serve each week.

Either way, repeat business means you score the client once and keep getting paid for months or years down the line.

So how do you introduce yourself?

It's as basic as driving around to law firms in your area and handing out business cards.

Of course, there's a right way to do it and a wrong way.

It's important not to think of this as selling.

You're not a commissioned salesmen peddling the latest copy machine or a subscription to the newspaper.

Sales people annoy the heck out of law firms, especially the legal secretaries and paralegals that staff the front desk.

The wrong way is coming in with a polished script and shiny postcards that scream, "Toss me in the recycling bin!"

Instead, it's a totally casual approach.

With no immediate commitment the pressure is lifted.

And it's amazing what can happen.

Like Bradley's story.

Bradley had never served papers before.

So he decided to start by visiting 10 law firms in Sun City, Arizona.

The first few were unproductive but he kept going.

Somewhere around the 4th or 5th firm he scored big.

The attorneys were practically jumping for joy to see him.

They had a huge case—13 separate papers—and were unhappy with their existing process server.

Not only did they hand Bradley 13 papers that day, but they went on to refer him to several other firms.

Bradley was ecstatic.

It's a great example of how finding just one client can springboard your success.

Be like Bradley.

He didn't have a fancy office or anything more than a basic understanding of civil process.

But he focused on the results, and found his first client in less time than it takes most newbies to file a small business license.

Bradley used a marketing packet—a business card stapled to the corner of a simple cover letter and rate sheet.

Here's an example cover letter (feel free to rip it off and adapt it for your business):

October 17th, 2018

Dear legal professional,

My name is Richard Young and I'm a local process server here in Denver.

I understand that finding a good process server can be tough. Problems range from high staff turnover to downright lousy attitude and customer service.

Here's what I offer:

   1) *A personal relationship: Your phone calls are answered or returned by me, not an answering service.*

2) *Accountability and trust: I'm responsible for every completed serve. Problems and concerns are handled directly, never passed off.*

3) *Friendly and efficient service: You relax. I handle the details. Simple online invoicing makes managing your bill a snap.*

Contact me directly at 303-555-0168 to see if we're a good fit.

Regards,

Richard Young

Include a basic letterhead and print it on standard white paper. Clean and modern is always more appealing than fancy design.

It's important to remember that some legal practices generate a lot more cases than others.

For your first pass I suggest targeting divorce attorneys.

Here's why:

1) Divorce attorneys are plentiful in most areas (just a reality in our modern society).

2) They generate a steady flow of papers to be served.

3) The defendants are easy to locate—the divorcing spouse can usually tell you where and when they work.

4) If the law firm doesn't arrange for service of process (usually the case with self-help legal offices) they're often open to referring their clients to you.

The market might vary in your area.

You could have more success with real estate attorneys, collection offices, landlords, or car dealerships.

But divorce attorneys are a great starting point.

You can always expand out from there.

Don't even waste your time with criminal attorneys. We're dealing only with civil cases and there's a clear distinction between criminal and civil attorneys.

Your initial goal should be to visit ten or twenty law firms in your area. By that point you should have several good leads or even one or two clients lined up.

Here's another big secret they're not going to tell you:

A surprising percentage of process servers are terrible at customer service.

Some are just, plain lazy or don't follow up with clients, others have the wannabe cop attitude I touched on earlier.

Savvy attorneys aren't buying it.

And process servers come and go.

There's always some new upstart or poorly-paid independent contractor ready to take the place of the last one. So don't be surprised that attorneys and paralegals keep one eye open for a reliable process server.

Present yourself well and they may give you a case or two to test the waters.

Your job is to prove yourself so indispensable they have no choice but to give you all of their work.

If you live in a big city, you already have an advantage because of the large number of law firms.

But if you live in a smaller city or town, consider teaming up with a process server in the nearest big city and exchanging work. Refer any work in the city to them and in exchange they refer any serves in your area back to you.

And don't despair, because even small towns have law firms.

Position yourself as the go-to process server in the local community.

Sometimes being a big fish in a small pond is a good thing —all the minnows you can eat and no sharks.

Marketing Your Business with a Website

For those of us who hate cold-calling and going door-to-door (myself included), promoting your business with a website is a great option.

These days, not having a website is the same as not being in business, because the majority of people looking for a process server will go straight to Google.

I strongly recommend building your website before printing up any business cards or marketing letters so that you can list your website's address on your marketing materials.

Either way, having a professional website boosts your image with potential clients and gives them a great way to contact you.

You might think it's tough to build a website, or that you need to hire a designer.

I'm here to tell you that's not the case.

It's never been easier to create a professional website, even with no experience or design skills.

While there are a lot of great platforms available for building your site, I recommend going straight to Site123 and getting started with their free plan.

There are a few things I like specifically about Site123:

1) The designs look awesome.

2) Answer a few quick questions about what kind of website you want and in less than 30 seconds it's up and running.

3) Everything is drag and drop from a simple dashboard. Want to display a photo? Just drag it into place. Same for headlines, icons, contact forms, maps, and client testimonials. Oh, and the layout, colors, and fonts are all selected with a couple of clicks.

4) Add a custom domain name and email address for a more professional appearance. No more Gmail or Yahoo.

5) Finally, you can build a fully functional website on the free plan and upgrade to a paid plan only when you're happy with the design.

To learn more, head over to:

https://www.processserver101.com/website

Promoting Your Website

The best part of having a website is that it's working for you, and available to potential clients, even when you take a day off.

But there are a few things you can do to make it easier for people searching Google to find your website.

Bookmark offers a built in blog, and by writing blog posts you increase your chances of being found.

Pay particular attention to keywords related to your town or city.

For example, if you live in Bakersfield and write a blog post about "process servers in Bakersfield," Google will index your posts and display it to people searching for related keywords.

It's not complicated, and it just takes a little effort to write a few blog posts and get them found on Google.

Another added benefit of blogging on your website is that it helps to establish your credibility, and tells potential clients that you're a valuable source of knowledge.

And if you really want to power up your website, you can add your business to Google My Business listings, so that's it's discovered on Google Search or Maps when people in your area search for process servers.

It's even free to create your listing, or you can buy paid ads for additional promotion.

To list your business, visit:

https://www.google.com/business

Business Cards

Once you have your business phone number setup through Google Voice and your website ready, it's time to order some business cards to hand out to friends, family, professional contacts, and potential clients.

Just like with your marketing letter and website theme, I recommend a clean, modern design that doesn't distract from your contact information.

There are a variety of online vendors that sell personalized business cards, or you can head to a local print shop, but I order all of my cards from Moo.

They're high-quality, offer great designs, and you can see exactly what your business cards will look like with their online customization tool:

https://www.moo.com

For more affordable option, you can also check out Vistaprint:

https://www.vistaprint.com

Associations & Networks

Some people enjoy networking.

They like the meetings, talking shop with others in their industry, and the inevitable drinking and socializing that occurs afterward.

I've never been one of those people, so I can't speak to the value of joining professional process server associations.

But I've met a few process servers who swear by it, and membership comes with the added benefit of getting listed in their professional directory. Some attorneys even turn to these directories when searching for a new process server.

In our industry, the largest professional organization is the National Association of Professional Process Servers:

https://napps.org

It's worth taking a look.

But I'd caution you against getting too wrapped up professional organizations until you're ready to take the next step in your business.

The fastest and most direct way to promote your business is to do it yourself, one client at a time.

That's probably why I've never joined an association.

I'm too busy staying focused on building my client list and growing my business.

Working With Clients

Your ability to work effectively with clients is just as important as your ability to promote yourself.

In fact, it's even more important.

Because one good client can be worth thousands of dollars in revenue (even tens of thousands).

Think about it:

What do you get from one serve, maybe $40-$150 depending on the market you're in?

Now imagine that same client gives you 10 papers to serve each week at a rate of $50 per serve.

10 papers x 52 weeks = $26,000 per year from a single client.

Focus on building strong relationships with your existing clients so they give you work over and over again, possibly for years to come.

And even better, happy clients will often refer you to their colleagues.

This is why I remind new process servers to be patient in the beginning.

It's tough when you're just starting out and the money isn't coming in, but if you can secure just a few good clients it's possible to build a real business with the potential to provide for you and your family.

Alternatively, if you're not taking care of the clients you manage to attract they're going to jump ship and take their business elsewhere, and you'll spend all of your time with your wheels spinning in the sand.

I'm reminded of Mark, a process server I used to work with a few years back.

He was a hustler.

And the guy knew how to get clients left and right (I think he'd even sold used cars for a few years before getting into the process server business).

He'd spend all day on the phone calling law firms, and when he was finished with a serve he'd drop in on nearby firms and work his magic.

It was great.

The business was coming in left and right, and it looked like there was a lot of money to be made.

But Mark had one fatal flaw.

He was terrible at working with the clients he'd already lined up.

He didn't return calls, didn't respond to their needs and concerns, and they'd begin to question their business relationship.

Of course, he'd make some small talk and smooth things over.

At least for a while.

But it didn't take long before they took their business to another process server, and Mark was back on the road hunting for new clients.

It was frustrating, because while Mark was great at bringing in new business, it was always slipping out of his fingers.

So what can you learn from Mark's story?

Two things:

1) Always over deliver with a new client, especially if it's your first client. This means serving the papers quickly, with as little hassle for the client as possible.

2) Stay in touch with your clients! Provide them with regular updates on their cases, particularly if it's a difficult serve and taking longer than usual (there are specialized apps for process server that make it easier than ever, but nothing beats a good old fashioned phone call).

Follow these two simple rules and you'll have clients giving you their business for a long time.

And in the end it's your bottom line that will benefit.

Billing & Payments

Part of working with clients is creating invoices and getting paid.

In our digital world, paper invoices just don't cut it. People are used to paying online with a few clicks, and making it easy for your clients to pay means you get paid faster.

If you do a quick Google search, you'll find quite a few websites that make it simple to bill your clients and get paid, but the one I use is called FreshBooks.

For a low monthly fee (starting at $15 a month as I write this), you can create professional invoices for each of your clients and accept credit cards with FreshBook's built-in payment processing.

There's no need for a separate merchant account or payment processor, and your clients will love the detailed invoices.

Here's the link:

https://www.freshbooks.com

The Future of Process Serving

The legal system in the United States has been largely consistent for hundreds of years, and the process server is a part of that system.

It's a field that won't disappear anytime soon.

But it's evolving to keep up with the times just like any other industry.

In the last few years, we've seen service of process via electronic means, such as email and even social media, become accepted by courts when other, more traditional methods of service have failed.

There was even a recent case in New York where service was made by Facebook.

While this is a new phenomenon, and personal service still accounts for the majority of serves made, it's wise for any savvy process server to keep an eye to the future.

It's likely more clients will request this type of service, and you may even consider specializing in alternative service to expand the revenue of your business.

But keep in mind that while non-traditional service is becoming more accepted, and will continue to grow in scale, the same rules apply:

Service must be made by a process server who is not a party to the case, who is legally authorized to serve process in their respective jurisdiction, and who will complete and file a return of service to the same standards as any case.

This means even with the changing landscape, the need for process servers won't disappear.

And instead of spending our time driving all over town drinking too much coffee and eating far too many donuts, we're more likely to find ourselves working from our laptops and iPads like a web developer or coder.

There will even be the opportunity to work remotely and in more than one state.

Can you imagine serving papers from home in your underwear or next to a beach somewhere?

It's coming sooner than you think.

Another point worth making is the new requirement springing up in places like New York that all serves are date, time, and GPS location stamped.

Courts have grown frustrated with the problem of sewer service and require more than just the process server's word that the papers were served correctly.

And there are some process servers complaining about this.

They see it as an intrusion into their business and a burdensome requirement.

But it's actually a way to protect yourself.

In fact, some process servers even mount a digital camera in their vehicle or wear a small body-cam to record their serves.

In the event you're questioned about the validity of a serve, wouldn't it be nice to have a way to prove you did the right thing?

Process Server Apps

As a response to the GPS requirements, a number of companies have developed apps for your smartphone that automate the process of recording your serves.

You can take a picture of the address where you made the serve, and the app will record the date, time, and the exact GPS coordinates of your location.

Even better, many will send an automatic email or text message notification to your client when service is complete.

Each app has its own advantages and disadvantages, so I'm listing a few of the more popular apps for you to compare and decide which works best for you:

PROOF
https://www.proofserve.com

ServeManager
https://www.servemanager.com

Paper Tracker
https://papertracker.biz

TriStar Software
https://tristarsoftware.com/process-server-software/

Fulcrum

https://www.fulcrumapp.com/apps/process-server/

Conclusion

If I could only leave you with one piece of advice it's not to get sidetracked by the small stuff.

Despite the wealth of information I've provided in this book, process serving at its core is a simple business.

Figure things out as you go.

Don't worry about what everyone else is doing.

And stay focused on finding your next client.

If you can do that, you'll build a business that will outlast the trends and provide for you and your family for a long time.

10-Step Getting Started Checklist

1) Research how to become a process server in your state and complete the requirements (if any).

2) Register your business and setup a local business bank account to accept payments.

3) Forward a free Google Voice office number to your smartphone.

4) Build a simple website to highlight your services and persuade clients that you're the right process server to handle their work.

5) Customize a marketing letter to distribute to attorneys and other potential clients.

6) Order a stack of shiny business cards (be sure to include your new office number and website address).

7) Visit law firms in your area, introduce yourself, and ask for work.

8) Repeat step #7 until you get your first gig.

9) Over-deliver on your first serve so they'll give you more business going forward.

10) Ask for referrals and continue to grow your business!

Recommended Resources

For handy reference, here's a quick list of the free and low-cost resources I've recommended throughout the book:

Process Server Legal Requirements
https://www.processserver101.com/process-server-laws

RocketLawyer Affidavit of Service Generator
https://www.rocketlawyer.com/document/affidavit-of-service.rl#/

Pipl Skip Tracing Search Engine
https://pipl.com

PAAPRS Safety Campaign
https://www.serve-now.com/resources/paaprs

Small Business Administration
https://www.sba.gov

Google Voice

https://voice.google.com

FaxBurner

https://www.faxburner.com

Site123 Website Builder

https://www.processserver101.com/website

Google My Business

https://www.google.com/business

Moo Business Cards

https://www.moo.com

Vistaprint Business Cards

https://www.vistaprint.com

National Association of Professional Process Servers

https://napps.org

FreshBooks Billing and Invoicing

https://www.freshbooks.com

PROOF

https://www.proofserve.com

ServeManager

https://www.servemanager.com

Paper Tracker

https://papertracker.biz

TriStar Software

https://tristarsoftware.com/process-server-software/

Fulcrum

https://www.fulcrumapp.com/apps/process-server/

State Associations

For those states with an active process server association, I've listed them below:

Arkansas Process Servers Association
http://arkansasprocessserversassociation.com

Arizona Process Servers Association
http://arizonaprocessservers.org

California Association of Legal Support Professionals
https://calspro.org

Process Server Association of Colorado
http://psaco.org

Florida Association of Professional Process Servers
https://www.fapps.org

Georgia Association of Professional Process Servers
http://gappsprocess.com

Illinois Association of Professional Process Servers
http://www.ilapps.com

Indiana Association of Professional Process Servers
http://inppsa.org

Mid Atlantic Association of Professional Process Servers
http://www.maapps.org

Mississippi Association of Professional Process Servers
http://mappsprocess.org

Michigan Court Officer, Deputy Sheriff and Process Servers Association
https://www.mcodsa.com

Minnesota Professional Process Servers Association
http://www.mnppsa.org

New Jersey Professional Process Servers Association
http://www.njppsa.org

New Mexico Process Servers Association
http://nmpsa.com

New York State Professional Process Servers Association
http://www.nysppsa.org

North Carolina Association of Professional Process Servers
http://ncapps.org

Oklahoma Private Process Server Association
https://okppsa.org

Oregon Association of Process Servers
http://www.oapsonline.com

Tennessee Association of Professional Process Servers
http://www.tntapps.org

Civil Process Servers Association of Texas
http://www.texasprocesswatch.com

Texas Process Servers Association
http://www.texasprocess.org

Utah Professional Association of Legal Services
http://www.upals.org

Commonwealth of Virginia Association of Professional Process Servers
http://www.covapps.org

Washington State Process Servers Association
http://wspsa.com

Author's Note

If you enjoyed this book and believe the information will be helpful for starting your own process server business, please consider leaving a review on Amazon.

Your review helps other people who may be looking for similar information, and who might also benefit from this book.

Wishing you the very best success,

Richard Young
https://www.processserver101.com

Disclaimer

The information in this book is published in good faith and for general information purposes only. Neither the author nor publisher make any warranties about the completeness, reliability, and accuracy of this information.

Any action you take upon the information in this book is strictly at your own risk.

Made in the USA
San Bernardino, CA
17 February 2020